The Mysterious
Miss

by Jo Cott
Illustrated by Bill Ledger

OXFORD
UNIVERSITY PRESS

In this story ...

Evan
(Flex)

Evan is super stretchy. He can stretch his body in any direction. He once stretched his arms all the way around Hero Academy.

Axel
(Invisiboy)

Miss Linen
(teacher)

Miss Baker
(dinner lady)

Mrs Butterworth
(cook)

Chapter 1:
Late homework

Miss Linen frowned. "Evan, where is your homework on super-materials?" she asked, flicking through the pile of workbooks in front of her.

It was nearly the end of the costumes lesson. Evan had been hoping the bell would go before Miss Linen realized his homework was missing.

He blushed. "Sorry – I ran out of time."

"This is the third time you've been late with your homework," said Miss Linen, with a sigh. "Starting today, I want you to go to the library every break until you get it done." With a wave of her hand, she made a workbook and a pen fly gently towards Evan.

"Yes, Miss Linen," said Evan, catching them.

At lunchtime, Evan met Axel in the dinner queue.

"Are you coming to play super-ball today?" asked Axel.

"I can't," Evan groaned. "I've got to do my homework in the library."

"Oh, bad luck," said Axel. "Maybe Miss Tula will help you. She's the new librarian." He rubbed his tummy. "Why is the queue so slow? I'm starving, and it's chocolate-mint pudding day!"

"Hi, Mrs Butterworth," said Evan, when he got to the front of the queue. "Are you all right?"

Mrs Butterworth's normally tidy hair was a mess, and there was a splodge of sauce on her cheek. She handed Evan some bread, a block of cheese and an apple.

"Miss Baker hasn't come in," she said. "I'm working on my own, so I haven't even had time to make pudding."

Behind him, Evan heard Axel wail, "Nooo! There's no chocolate-mint pudding?"

"Is Miss Baker ill?" Evan asked.

Mrs Butterworth replied, "I've no idea. I left her to tidy and lock up last night, but the kitchen was in a terrible state this morning. Pots and pans all over the place! She's normally so tidy. I'm worried about her."

Evan went to find a seat. "Where could Miss Baker be?" he wondered.

Chapter 2:
Miss Tula

Evan pushed open the door to the library.

"Hello?" he called, walking down the middle of the room. "Anyone here? Miss Tula?"

There was a soft thump from behind him, and then a voice said, "Shhh! Quiet in the library."

Evan turned, startled. A small woman with purple hair and yellow glasses was looking at him.

"I didn't hear you coming," Evan said.

Miss Tula smiled. "Librarians are always quiet. Can I help you?"

"I've got to finish my homework," Evan admitted. "It's a bit late."

"Oh dear," said Miss Tula. The light glinted off her glasses as she pulled out a chair. "You can sit here."

"Thanks," said Evan, sitting down. He pulled a bag of peppermints out of his rucksack. "Would you like one of these, Miss Tula?"

Miss Tula jumped back, almost crashing into a bookshelf. "Get those away from me!" she hissed.

Evan's eyebrows shot up in surprise.

Miss Tula took a deep, shaky breath. "Sorry. It's just … I'm allergic to peppermint."

Evan stared as the librarian hurried away. He'd never heard of anyone with an allergy to peppermint before.

Evan tried to work, but he started thinking about Miss Baker again. She was always in school, every day. What could have kept her away?

Then, out of the corner of his eye, he saw something move high up on the ceiling. Evan jerked his head upwards, but there was nothing there ... just a lot of cobwebs.

Chapter 3:
Cobwebs

Suddenly, Axel appeared out of thin air directly in front of Evan's desk.

"Aaaah!" shrieked Evan, falling off his chair.

"Sorry!" said Axel.

"People keep making me jump today," said Evan, rubbing his bumped elbow.

Axel helped Evan back on to his chair. "How are you getting on with your homework?"

"I don't know where to start," Evan said with a sigh. "I don't know what makes the best super-material."

"Spiders," said Axel.

"Huh?" Evan replied.

"The silk they spin their webs with is incredible stuff. It's super-strong."

Evan shuddered. "I don't like spiders."

"This is the book you need," said Axel, pulling one off the shelf. "Miss Tula found it for me when I was doing my homework."

The book had a large picture of a spider on the front cover.

Evan gulped. "Thanks."

"No problem. See you later!" Axel waved, and then he turned invisible again.

Evan started reading. He found out that spider silk was one of the strongest materials in the natural world. However, for some reason, spiders didn't like peppermint. "Just like Miss Tula," Evan thought.

He was just about to start writing down some useful facts when the bell went. Break time was over. He sighed and put the book back on the shelf. He'd have to come back later.

At supper time that evening, the dinner hall was in chaos again. This time, Magnus the caretaker was behind the food counter, looking hot and bothered. A spoon was sticking out of his top pocket, and he had spaghetti in his hair. He gave Evan a plate of pasta with a fried egg on top.

Evan looked at it doubtfully.

"It's the best I could do," said Magnus. "First Miss Baker goes missing, now Mrs Butterworth. I had to step in and make dinner at the last minute."

Evan's mouth fell open in shock. Miss Baker and Mrs Butterworth were *both* missing? "Where could they be?" he asked.

"Nobody knows," said Magnus. He looked around and lowered his voice. "The Department for the Management of Superpowers is sending someone to investigate."

When Evan got to the library that evening, there was no sign of Miss Tula either.

"Miss Tula! I'm back!" he called, but there was no answer. Had the librarian gone missing too?

"I shouldn't jump to conclusions," Evan told himself. "Maybe she's just in the storeroom." He went over to the door and pushed it open.

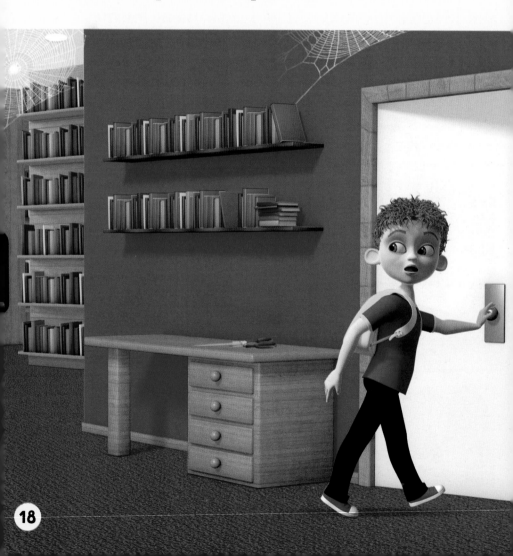

The room was *full* of cobwebs. The silk strands
stretched from floor to ceiling, covering everything in
sticky, silver threads.

Then Evan gasped as he saw something else. Right
in the middle of the room, trapped in spider silk ...
were Miss Baker and Mrs Butterworth!

Chapter 4:
The spider

Evan couldn't believe his eyes. "Miss Baker!" he called.

Miss Baker turned her head. "Evan?"

"I'll get you out," called Evan. He started to clamber between the sticky threads, his heart thumping. What kind of spider could spin a web this big?

"No, Evan!" cried Mrs Butterworth. "Go and get help before she comes back!"

"Who?" Evan asked.

There was a scuttling noise above Evan, and he froze. He looked up and gasped.

Miss Tula was on the ceiling! Instead of two legs, she now had six, and her feet moved easily across the smooth surface as she stared down at him. She looked like … a spider!

"You had to go poking your nose in, didn't you, Evan?" Miss Tula said.

Terrified, Evan turned and ran out of the storeroom, his rucksack bumping against his back.

Miss Tula scurried across the ceiling after him. Sticky threads shot through the air, gluing Evan's feet to the floor.

"I won't let you spoil my plan!" she hissed at him. "I've spent months working out how to get my own back on Hero Academy!"

"Help!" shouted Evan.

Miss Tula scowled. "Shh! Quiet in the library!"

Evan looked towards the library door, but it was shut. He reached out an arm. It grew longer and longer as he stretched towards the door. If he could just open it …

"Oh no you don't," said the spider-librarian. She sealed the door shut with a jet of silk, and then dropped down from the ceiling to land just in front of Evan. "Want to know my first name?" She began to wrap spider silk round and round his legs. "It's Taran … *Taran Tula.*"

Miss Tula

Catchphrase: Shh!
Hobbies: climbing, weaving.
Likes: books, flies,
things with eight legs,
like octopuses or two
chairs stuck together.
Dislikes: peppermints,
knots in her webs.
Beware! Miss Tula is
half human, half spider.
She moves very quietly
so you might not
hear her sneak up
on you.

Evan tried to think. The spider silk was too strong for him to break. In another moment, he'd be trapped like Miss Baker and Mrs Butterworth. He looked around desperately. On the shelf, he spotted the book Axel had shown him. The one about spiders … and their dislike of peppermint.

His rucksack was still on his back, but for Evan's
elastic arms that was no problem. He pulled out the
bag of peppermints. "Miss Tula!" he said bravely.
"I've got a treat for you."

"What?" Miss Tula looked up, and Evan rolled a
peppermint towards her.

"AAARGHHH!" Miss Tula cried. Instantly,
she stopped spinning silk around Evan's legs
and scuttled backwards.

Evan quickly threw more peppermints across the floor to force Miss Tula into a corner.

While the librarian was distracted, Evan reached over to her desk for a pair of scissors.

SNIP! He cut through the silk, and his legs were free.

Evan ran over to the library door. *SNIP!* The door was free. He flung it open and shouted, "Help! In here, quickly!"

He knew it wouldn't take long for help to reach him.

Next, Evan ran back to the storeroom to release Miss Baker and Mrs Butterworth.

"You hero!" cried Miss Baker. "I'll make extra chocolate-mint pudding for you."

"Did someone say chocolate-mint pudding?" said Axel, appearing in the library. His jaw dropped with surprise. "What happened here?"

"Your book saved me!" Evan told him. "I'll tell you later."

"Gosh!" cried Miss Linen, running in. "Look at all this wonderful spider silk! I could use this to strengthen your super suits."

"You can have it," Evan told her. "It came from *her*." He nodded towards the whimpering librarian. "She kidnapped Miss Baker and Mrs Butterworth."

Miss Linen looked disapprovingly at Miss Tula. "Why did you do this?" she demanded.

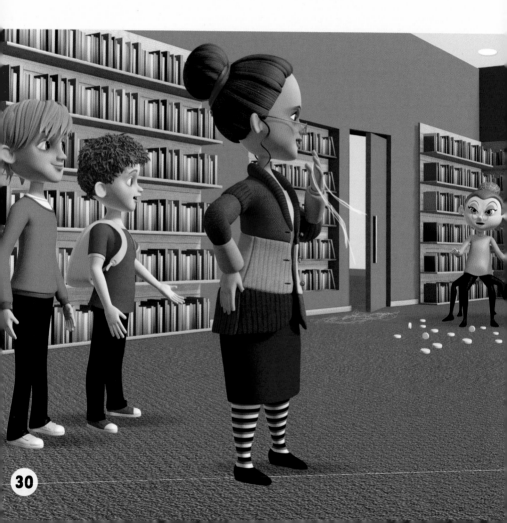

"You don't remember me, do you?" Miss Tula hissed. "When I was a spiderling, I was a pupil at Hero Academy, but I had to leave."

"Why?" asked Evan.

"The terrible, horrible chocolate-mint pudding of course! Every Wednesday without fail, we had chocolate-mint pudding. Urgh!" She pulled a face. "Even the smell ... I couldn't take it. I could have been a great superhero!"

"Well, the inspector from the Department of the Management of Superpowers can deal with you now," Miss Linen said sternly. "Evan, thanks to you, the school is saved!"

Miss Tula groaned in disappointment.

"Er, Miss Linen?" asked Evan. "Does this mean ..."

"... that you don't have to do your homework?" Miss Linen finished for him. She smiled. "Of course you still have to do your homework, Evan. I expect it on my desk first thing tomorrow!"